BOSTON
CELTICS

by Marty Gitlin

Published by ABDO Publishing Company, 8000 West 78th Street, Edina, Minnesota 55439. Copyright © 2012 by Abdo Consulting Group, Inc. International copyrights reserved in all countries. No part of this book may be reproduced in any form without written permission from the publisher. SportsZone™ is a trademark and logo of ABDO Publishing Company.

Printed in the United States of America,
North Mankato, Minnesota
062011
092011

 THIS BOOK CONTAINS AT LEAST 10% RECYCLED MATERIALS.

Editor: Alex Monnig
Copy Editor: Anna Comstock
Series design and cover production: Christa Schneider
Interior production: Carol Castro

Photo Credits: Mary Schwalm/AP Images, cover; Dick Raphael/NBAE/Getty Images, 1; AP Images, 4, 8, 10, 13, 14, 17, 21, 23, 25, 26, 33, 42 (top), 42 (middle), 42 (bottom); CR/AP Images, 7; J. Walter Green/AP Images, 18; Liss/AP Images, 29, 43 (top); Peter Southwick/AP Images, 30; Lawrence Jackson/AP Images, 34; Steven Senne/AP Images, 37, 43 (bottom); Michael Dwyer/AP Images, 39; Winslow Townson/AP Images, 40, 43 (middle); Mark Lennihan/AP Images, 44; Robert E. Klein/AP Images, 47

Library of Congress Cataloging-in-Publication Data
Gitlin, Marty.
  Boston Celtics / by Marty Gitlin.
     p. cm. -- (Inside the NBA)
  Includes index.
  ISBN 978-1-61783-150-8
  1. Boston Celtics (Basketball team)--History--Juvenile literature. I. Title.
  GV885.52.B67G58 2011
  796.323'640974461--dc22
                              2011012358

TABLE OF CONTENTS

CHAPTER 1

THE GREATEST GAME EVER?

Elated fans at the Boston Garden chanted, "We're number one! We're number one! We're number one!" They had a right to be excited. Their Boston Celtics had taken a 109–106 lead in the second overtime of Game 5 of the 1976 National Basketball Association (NBA) Finals.

A win over the Phoenix Suns would place the Celtics on the verge of their second championship in three years.

But the fans were not screaming for long. The Suns scored two quick baskets to forge ahead 110–109. With just a few seconds remaining, legendary Celtics forward John Havlicek dribbled toward the basket and shot the ball. Boston fans held their breath as the ball soared toward the hoop. When it banged off the backboard and swished through the

Dave Cowens (18) tries to score during Boston's 98–87 victory over the Phoenix Suns in Game 1 of the 1976 NBA Finals.

THE HUSTLER

Dave Cowens was one of the hardest workers in the NBA. His hustle earned him a place in the Basketball Hall of Fame. Cowens was undersized for a center at only 6 feet 9 inches tall, but he remained in constant motion. He blocked shots, rebounded, was a tremendous passer, and played tenacious defense. "I thought he was a wild man," teammate Paul Silas said.

Cowens averaged between 16 and 21 points and 14 and 16 rebounds per game every season from 1970 through 1978. He made the All-Star team seven straight years. And he was named NBA Most Valuable Player (MVP) in 1973 after averaging career highs in points (20.5) and rebounds (16.2). As a coach, Cowens guided the Charlotte Hornets to the playoffs in 1997 and 1998. He was inducted into the Hall of Fame in 1991.

net, the fans once again went wild. The Celtics had won the title. Or so they thought.

Little did they know, the game had not yet ended. The officials decided that there was still one second left on the clock. The Celtics had already started celebrating in their locker room. But they had to return to the floor. And the fans who had rushed onto the floor had to return to their seats.

It appeared the Suns had no chance to win. They had the ball under their own basket. And scoring in one second from the opposite side of the floor seemed impossible. But Phoenix guard Paul Westphal had an idea. He called for a timeout even though the Suns had no timeouts left. That was a technical foul. The Celtics were awarded a foul shot. Guard Jo Jo White made the

Celtics guard Jo Jo White made the All-Star team seven times and was named MVP of the 1976 NBA Finals

free throw to give his team a 112–110 lead. But this sequence of events also gave the Suns the ball at midcourt. And they were only down by one basket.

Still, scoring was still a long shot for Phoenix. And, indeed, Suns forward Garfield Heard launched a long shot. Incredibly, it went high into the air and fell through the hoop to tie

Wonderful White

There was one player on which the Celtics teams of the 1970s could always depend. That player was guard Jo Jo White. White played in all of Boston's games from 1972 to 1977. He never averaged less than 18.1 points per game during that time. And he rose to the occasion when the Celtics needed him the most. The seven-time All-Star was named MVP in Boston's 1976 NBA Finals victory over the Phoenix Suns.

Boston bench player Glenn McDonald (30) scored six important points for the Celtics in the third overtime of Game 5 of the 1976 NBA Finals.

Angering Auerbach

Celtics owner John Y. Brown made general manager Red Auerbach mad in 1979. Brown traded three first-round NBA Draft picks to the New York Knicks for aging forward Bob McAdoo without asking Auerbach. "He made one great big deal that could have destroyed the team, without even consulting me," Auerbach later said. "He did ruin it. . . . One guy can ruin it so fast your head will swim." McAdoo played just 20 games with the Celtics before they dealt him to the Detroit Pistons.

the score at 112–112. The game was headed to a third overtime.

The stunning basket by Heard could have doomed the Celtics. Dave Cowens, Charlie Scott, and Paul Silas, three of the team's stars, were on the bench after fouling out. But unlikely hero Glenn McDonald scored six points in the third overtime, including the game-winning basket.

When the game finally concluded that June evening, the Celtics had emerged with a 128–126 victory. Many believe it was the greatest playoff game in NBA history.

"I personally would have to say it was one of the greatest games, and I was very happy to be a part of it," White said. "It was draining. It was strenuous. You had to reach down for everything you had to pull out a victory. It had all the dramatics that anyone could ask for."

The deciding Game 6 was played in Phoenix. Boston won 87–80 to clinch the championship.

The Celtics are one of the NBA's most storied and successful franchises. They have won 17 championships—more than any other team. And they have produced some of the best players in NBA history. But the 1976 title, and the one

Good Player, Great Coach

Don Nelson contributed nicely to the great Celtics teams of the 1960s and 1970s. The forward played in nearly all their games from 1965 to 1976. He averaged at least 10 points per contest in nine of those seasons. But Nelson was even better as a coach. He guided four teams to a combined 1,335 victories through the 2009–10 season. At that time, he had won more games than any coach in NBA history, although he never won a title. Nelson coached the Golden State Warriors in the 2009–10 season, but he was fired just before the start of the next season.

before it in 1974, sat between two extended eras of greatness. The dynasty of the 1950s and 1960s led by Bill Russell was over. It would be several years before Larry Bird led a Boston revival in the 1980s. The rest of the 1970s would be rather disappointing for the Celtics and their fans.

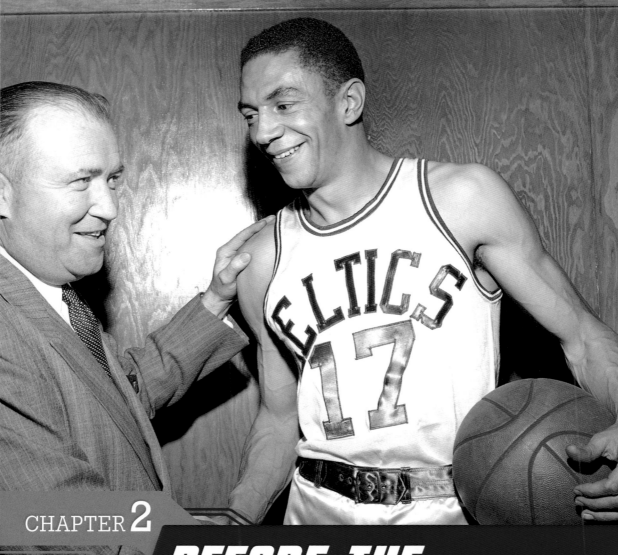

CHAPTER 2

BEFORE THE DYNASTY

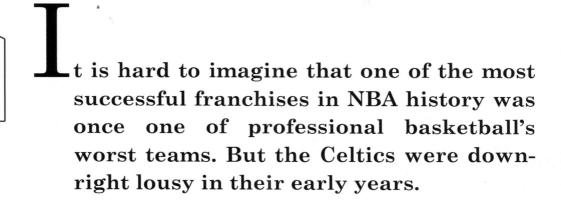

It is hard to imagine that one of the most successful franchises in NBA history was once one of professional basketball's worst teams. But the Celtics were downright lousy in their early years.

The Celtics were among the 11 teams that formed the original Basketball Association of America (BAA) for the 1946–47 season. Celtics owner Walter Brown was one of the founding members of the BAA. He also ran the Boston Garden, the arena in which the Celtics played their home games.

Brown certainly was not happy with how the Celtics performed under coach John Russell. The team finished its first season with a 22–38 record and tied for last place

Celtics owner Walter Brown, *left*, always tried to bring in new players such as Don Barksdale, *right*, to make the team better.

in the Eastern Division. They improved a bit the next season and even won a playoff game against the Chicago Stags. For the 1948–49 campaign, Brown brought in a host of new players and a new coach, Alvin Julian. But the results were the same. Boston posted a 25–35 mark.

The BAA merged with the National Basketball League (NBL) in 1949 to form the NBA. That certainly did not help the hapless Celtics. They sported a 22–46 record and ended their first season in the NBA in last place. But Boston got lucky when six NBA teams folded the following season. Those teams' players were either signed or drafted by other teams.

The Celtics ended up with center Ed Macauley and rookie guard Bob Cousy. They also hired Red Auerbach as their new coach. Auerbach had coached the Washington Capitols in the BAA and the Tri-Cities Blackhawks during the first NBA season.

Cousy opened the eyes of fans, teammates, and opposing players. He was a wizard with the basketball. He dazzled everyone with behind-the-back dribbles and by looking one way and passing the ball another. He did not even shoot a jump shot. He preferred to drive to the basket and push the ball into the air with one hand. His unique style nearly scared away Auerbach.

Bob Cousy (14) goes after a loose ball in a February 1956 game against the St. Louis Hawks.

"Red wasn't too sure he wanted Cousy," Celtics guard Kenny Sailors said. "[Cousy] was kind of a Fancy Dan. He was a great dribbler, but he pulled some stuff that the old-timers didn't go for. Oh boy, it worked out for both of them, though."

It certainly did. The additions of Auerbach, Cousy, and Macauley turned the Celtics into winners. During the

Player and Entertainer

Forward Tony Lavelli did not just play basketball for the Celtics in the late 1940s. He also played the accordion for the team's fans. In one game in 1949, he scored 23 of his 26 points in the second half. That was after he played several songs for the crowd on his accordion at halftime. Lavelli was also known for his deadly long-range hook shot. His cousin, Dante Lavelli, was a star wide receiver for the Cleveland Browns of the National Football League (NFL).

Celtics center Ed Macauley (22) blocks a shot by the Knicks' Nat Clifton (8) during a 1955 game.

1950–51 season, Macauley led Boston with 20.4 points and 9.1 rebounds per game. Cousy averaged 15.6 points per game and ranked fourth in the NBA in assists with 341 his rookie year. His speed and passing ability allowed the Celtics to play a fast-paced style in which they ran up and down the floor.

The result was their first winning season and the team's first trip to the NBA playoffs. Three more winning seasons followed. By that time, Cousy was paired at the other guard spot with sharpshooter and future Hall of Famer Bill Sharman.

There was just one problem. The Celtics were weak on defense. That flaw doomed them in the playoffs year after year. They lost to the New York Knicks in the first round in 1951 and 1952, and in the second round in 1953. They fell to the Syracuse Nationals in the second round in 1954 and 1955, and in the first round in 1956.

During the 1954–55 season, the Celtics became the first team in NBA history to average more than 100 points per game. But their inability to stop other teams prevented them from winning titles. So Auerbach traded Macauley and future star Cliff Hagan to the St. Louis Hawks. In return,

GREEN TEAM LED BY RED

Red Auerbach is known for his extraordinary success coaching the Celtics from 1950 to 1966. But his desire to use only the best players, regardless of skin color, set the tone for integration in the NBA.

In 1950, Auerbach selected Chuck Cooper, the first African-American player in the NBA Draft. Auerbach was also the first to hire an African-American head coach when he chose Bill Russell to take over the team before the 1966–67 season.

Auerbach is considered one of the best coaches in NBA history. He led the Celtics to a glorious run of success in the 1950s and 1960s. He finished his career with a 938–479 record.

Auerbach continued his connection with the Celtics—serving as general manager, team president, and vice chairman of the board—until his death in 2006.

Boston received Bill Russell, a 6-foot-9 rookie center from the University of San Francisco.

Auerbach was seeking a strong defender in the middle. What he got in Russell was perhaps the greatest defensive player to ever grace an NBA floor. Russell was a high-jumper and hurdler on his high school track team. He could leap high to grab rebounds and block shots. But he could do much more. Author Lew Freedman wrote:

"Russell was a vacuum cleaner [as a rebounder] and brilliant at throwing a two-handed outlet pass to jump-start fast breaks. Before Russell, the NBA's tallest players swatted . . . shots out of play. . . . Russell jumped, blocked the shot, then caught the ball on the way down. He swooped down . . . and plagued their thoughts and shots. He intimidated them with his agility and [stare].

"Opponents grew [worried] that Russell would appear like some wide-winged bird to ruin their shots. . . . Cousy said he couldn't begin to count the number of times he heard someone say, 'Russell came out of nowhere!' He was just quicker than anyone else."

The 1956 NBA Draft netted two other future Hall of Famers in forward Tom Heinsohn and guard K. C. Jones. The Celtics were about to thrive. Winning NBA championships would soon become an annual event.

Bill Russell, *center*, pulls down a rebound during an April 1959 game against the Minneapolis Lakers.

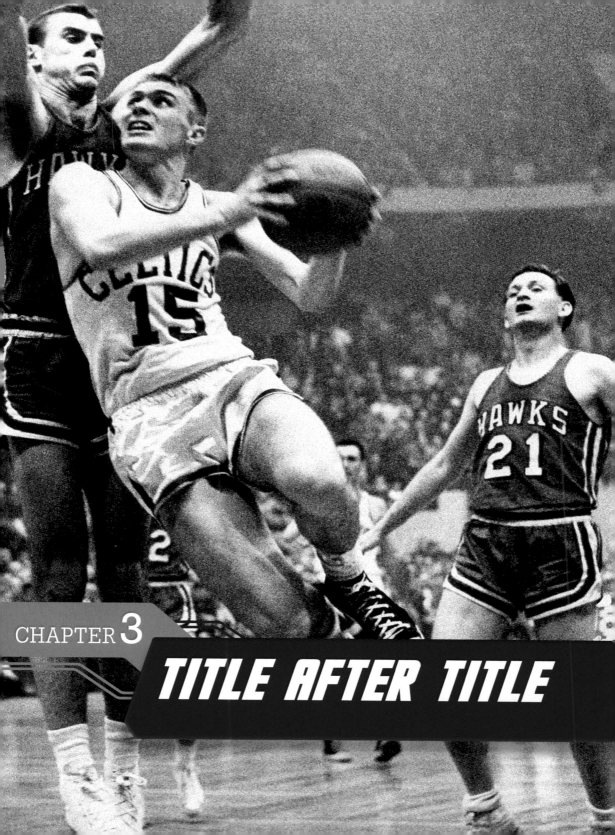

CHAPTER 3

TITLE AFTER TITLE

Heading into the 1956–57 season, the Celtics had never reached the NBA Finals. Few believed they would achieve that goal with such a young team.

Forward Tom Heinsohn and center Bill Russell were talented players. But most thought it would take time for them to make a huge impact.

They thought wrong. Heinsohn was named NBA Rookie of the Year. And Russell averaged an incredible 20 rebounds per game. Their veteran teammate, point guard Bob Cousy, earned league MVP honors. The Celtics finished the season in first place with a 44–28 record. They then avenged their previous playoff losses to the Syracuse Nationals with a three-game sweep to reach the 1957 Finals against the St. Louis Hawks.

The teams split the first six games to force a showdown for the championship. Game 7 was tied in the final moments of

In 1957, Tom Heinsohn (15) won the NBA Rookie of the Year Award and helped the Celtics reach the NBA Finals for the first time.

the second overtime. Forward Jim Loscutoff hit two foul shots to give the host Celtics a 125–123 lead. When a last-second shot by Hawks star forward Bob Pettit bounced off the rim, the Celtics had their first NBA title. They had won even though Cousy and Bill Sharman combined to miss 35 of their 40 shots. The team celebrated by shaving Russell's beard in the locker room.

"My nervous system is shot," Red Auerbach said. "This is a great team. The fellows refused to quit, and finally came through. This is a great day."

The 1957–58 season would not be so great, although the Celtics still made it to the Finals. Once there, however, Boston lost to St. Louis four games to two. Russell was named NBA regular-season MVP, but he hurt his ankle in the Finals.

The Celtics then embarked on one of the greatest title runs in NBA history. During their eight-year championship dynasty, which spanned from 1959 to 1966, they established two heated rivalries. One was against the Philadelphia Warriors, who later moved to San Francisco. The other was against the Minneapolis Lakers, who would relocate to Los Angeles.

An intense personal rivalry was also forged in the early 1960s. It was between

Sam Jones played his entire 12-year career with the Celtics. He helped the team win 10 championships and was a five-time All-Star.

Russell and 7-foot-1 center Wilt Chamberlain, who played for the Warriors, the Philadelphia 76ers, and the Lakers. Chamberlain, the fourth leading scorer in NBA history, was frustrated time and again by Russell's brilliant defense. With Russell leading the way, the Celtics beat Chamberlain's teams in the Eastern Conference finals in 1960, 1962, 1965, 1966, and 1968, and for the NBA title in 1964 and 1969.

One of the most exciting clashes between the two big men was in 1965. Russell's Celtics and Chamberlain's 76ers traded wins in the first six games of the Eastern

Conference finals. The host Celtics led by seven points with two minutes left in Game 7. But Chamberlain scored six quick points to cut the lead to 110–109. Russell then committed a turnover, giving Philadelphia a chance to win. The 76ers' Hal Greer tossed the ball toward teammate Chet Walker, but Celtic John Havlicek tipped it away and teammate Sam Jones grabbed the ball.

That is when legendary Celtics radio broadcaster Johnny Most made one of the most famous calls in NBA history.

"Havlicek steals it!" Most yelled as his voice reached a fever pitch. "Havlicek stole the ball! It's all over! Johnny Havlicek is being mobbed by the fans. It's all over! . . . Oh boy, what a play by Havlicek at the end of this ballgame! . . . A spectacular series comes to

Heinsohn Gets His Due

Tom Heinsohn sometimes did not receive the recognition he deserved. But he did win eight NBA championships in the nine seasons he played with the Celtics. From 1956 to 1965, the 6-foot-7 forward averaged 18.6 points and 8.8 rebounds per game. However, he was often overlooked because of his more talented teammates. Heinsohn went on to coach the Celtics to titles in 1974 and 1976. He was finally inducted into the Hall of Fame in 1986.

an end in spectacular fashion! John Havlicek is being hoisted aloft. . . . He yells and waves his hands. Bill Russell wants to grab Havlicek! He hugs him! He squeezes John Havlicek!"

The Celtics clinched the championship by easily defeating the Los Angeles Lakers in the 1965 NBA Finals. But no dynasty lasts forever. Heinsohn retired. Auerbach announced that he would quit as coach after the 1965–66 season. And

Bill Russell, *left*, tries to block Wilt Chamberlain's shot during Game 7 of the 1969 NBA Finals. The Celtics won 108–106.

Russell and standout guard K. C. Jones had celebrated their 30th birthdays and were also nearing the end of their playing careers.

Auerbach went out in style. His team beat the Lakers again for its eighth straight NBA title in 1966. As Boston's general manager, he named Russell as his replacement. Russell would be both a player and the coach, becoming the first African-American head coach in major American sports history. And though his Celtics

CELTICS' SUPER SIXTH MAN

Coach Red Auerbach took pride in having at least one excellent player who did not start. That player was the Celtics' sixth man and was generally good enough to star on other teams.

The best-known sixth man in Celtics history was John Havlicek. He came off the bench through much of his career. But he was on the court in close games in the fourth quarter when the Celtics needed him the most.

The 6-foot-5 Havlicek played guard and forward in the NBA. He was an All-Star for 13 straight years starting in 1966. He averaged at least 20 points per game in eight straight seasons. And he contributed to eight league championships.

Havlicek peaked during the 1970–71 season. He averaged career highs in points (28.9), rebounds (9.0), and assists (7.5) per game.

did not win the title in 1967, he guided them to NBA Finals victories over the Lakers in 1968 and 1969. Russell retired from playing and stepped down from his coaching position after the second of those titles. The Celtics had won 11 championships in 13 years—the most dominant stretch in league history.

During that remarkable period, Russell led the NBA in rebounding five seasons. Cousy won four of his eight NBA assist titles during that stretch. Both were elected into the Hall of Fame. So were other Celtics of that era, including Auerbach, Havlicek, Heinsohn, Sam Jones, K. C. Jones, and Sharman.

But the Celtics' dynasty was not about any individual. It was about outstanding team basketball. It was about every player working together

Fans carry John Havlicek off the court after his deflection at the end of Game 7 of the 1965 Eastern Conference finals.

on offense and defense. It was about performing their best with NBA championships on the line.

All good things eventually must come to an end. And the Celtics' incredible run of success was no different. Although the 1970s would still provide some excitement, it was not until the selection of Larry Bird in the 1978 NBA Draft that the Celtics would start another extended run of excellence.

CHAPTER 4

FLYING BACK TO THE TOP WITH BIRD

The 1970s would not be filled with championship after championship for Boston. The team fell just short of the NBA Finals three times, losing in the Eastern Conference finals in 1972, 1973, and 1975. But they were still able to win two titles during the decade.

They beat the Milwaukee Bucks four games to three for the 1974 championship. Two years later, in 1976, the Celtics triumphed over the Phoenix Suns four games to two.

After the 1976 title, the team went through a bad stretch. Paul Silas was traded in 1976. Coach Tom Heinsohn, whose leadership on the bench had helped the team earn the two championships in the 1970s, was fired in 1978. John Havlicek retired that same year. A series of poor college draft picks prevented the Celtics from improving. They suffered through two straight losing seasons. In 1978–79,

Dave Cowens jumps to block a pass from the Cleveland Cavaliers' Jim Brewer during Game 5 of the 1976 Eastern Conference finals.

their record was just 29–53. Sportswriters and opposing players were even claiming that the Celtics were not trying hard enough on the court. "The Celtics used to stand for something," *Boston Globe* writer Bob Ryan said. "Now all they stand for is the [national] anthem."

However, they were once again about to stand for greatness when one of the top players in NBA history arrived in Boston. That player was Larry Bird. Boston had gambled by taking Bird in the 1978 NBA Draft. Nobody knew whether the high-scoring junior forward would return to Indiana State University for his senior year. If the Celtics selected Bird and he chose to remain in school, it could have been a wasted pick.

Team after team passed on Bird as the NBA Draft began. They were worried about him

Hail McHale

Even Larry Bird could not over-shadow the greatness of Kevin McHale. The Celtics grabbed the 6-foot-10 forward with the third over-all pick of the 1980 NBA Draft. They never regretted it. McHale averaged 17.9 points and 7.3 rebounds per game during his 13 seasons in the NBA, all with Boston. He twice led the league in field-goal percentage by making more than 60 percent of his shots. The Hall of Famer later served as general manager and coach of the Minnesota Timberwolves and in 2011 was named coach of the Houston Rockets.

staying in college for another year. Boston's general manager Red Auerbach eventually selected Bird with the sixth overall pick. He believed Bird would want to play for one of the NBA's most storied franchises. Bird instead decided to finish his career at Indiana State.

The story had a happy ending for the Celtics, though. Bird could have entered the

Larry Bird, *right*, poses with Red Auerbach after joining the Celtics in 1979. Bird went on to win the Rookie of the Year Award.

NBA Draft again in 1979, but he chose to sign a contract with Boston for $650,000 per year. At the time, it was more money than any rookie in any sport had ever earned. Neither Bird nor the Celtics would regret it.

Bird exploded onto the NBA scene. The 6-foot-9 forward was better than the NBA's other rookies in all areas of the game. He was an excellent passer and rebounder, and his feathery shooting touch helped him become one of the NBA's top scorers. Bird averaged 21 points and 10 rebounds per game his first season. And he was named league Rookie of the Year.

Meanwhile, the Celtics were building a winning team in the late 1970s and early 1980s. They hired Bill Fitch, a highly respected coach who had coached the Cleveland

Larry Bird, *right*, and the Celtics battled rival Magic Johnson, *left*, and the Lakers in the NBA Finals three times in the 1980s.

Cavaliers for nine seasons. They also drafted talented forwards Cedric "Cornbread" Maxwell and Kevin McHale, and guard Danny Ainge. They traded for center Robert Parish, a strong scorer and rebounder, and consistent guard Dennis Johnson. All could score and play defense.

The Celtics were about to embark on a second era of excellence. And just as Bill Russell had forged an intense rivalry with Wilt Chamberlain, Bird would start one with Los Angeles Lakers point guard Magic Johnson. Their rivalry began when Johnson's Michigan State University team beat Bird's Indiana State team in the 1979 college championship game. Bird and Johnson's rivalry would also play a significant factor in the NBA's increased popularity in the 1980s.

In 1981, Bird helped the Celtics defeat the Houston Rockets four games to two for the NBA championship. After a lull in the late 1970s, Boston was back on top of the basketball world.

In 1984, Bird won the first of his three consecutive league MVP awards. The Celtics advanced to the NBA Finals against the Lakers. The teams had not competed against each other for a championship since 1969. The Celtics had won all seven previous Finals meetings. But Johnson's Lakers had captured two league crowns since then, in 1980 and 1982. Many basketball followers believed that Los Angeles had a dynasty in the making.

The teams split the first six games. When Game 7

Capping Great Careers

Three of the finest players in NBA history played with the Celtics toward the end of their careers. Guards Pete Maravich and Nate "Tiny" Archibald and center Bill Walton were All-Star players well before they arrived in Boston. Maravich, a brilliant scorer and passer, played 26 games with the Celtics during the 1979–80 season. Archibald was a Celtic from 1978 to 1983. And Walton was with Boston from 1985 to 1987. He helped the team win the 1986 title as a reserve player after leading the Portland Trail Blazers to a championship nine years earlier.

approached, Maxwell told his teammates, "Just hop on my back, and I'll take you in." Maxwell racked up 24 points, eight rebounds, and eight assists in a 111–102 Celtics home victory. When it was over, Auerbach crowed to the media.

"You guys were talking about a dynasty the Lakers had," Auerbach said. "But

TWO TRAGEDIES

One of the worst moments in Celtics franchise history occurred in 1986, when Len Bias suddenly died. The Celtics had drafted the University of Maryland star forward with the second overall pick in the 1986 NBA Draft. Bias appeared thrilled when he posed for pictures wearing a green Celtics cap. But two days later, the forward died of a drug overdose. The Celtics and the entire nation were shocked. Bias had passed a drug test just three weeks earlier.

"That was one of the biggest disappointments of my career because, in my honest opinion, he was not a [drug addict]," Red Auerbach said. "He was a super kid."

Tragedy struck again in the summer of 1993 when Celtics guard Reggie Lewis collapsed and died from heart complications while shooting baskets. Lewis had developed into one of the top scorers in the NBA.

what dynasty? Here's the only dynasty right here."

But Auerbach was wrong about the Celtics. And the media was wrong about the Lakers. Both teams were so good that neither could dominate. The Lakers broke their streak of eight NBA Finals defeats to the Celtics. They beat them for the championship in 1985. But the Celtics rebounded the next year. They finished the 1985–86 season with a 67–15 mark, including a 40–1 record at home. Bird and McHale combined to average 47 points per game. Boston lost just three playoff games, including two to Houston, before dispatching the Rockets in the 1986 Finals.

But just as the first era of greatness ended, so did the second. Boston lost to the Lakers in the 1987 NBA Finals. Then they slipped into

Kevin McHale, *left*, slam dunks against Hakeem Olajuwon of the Houston Rockets in Game 6 of the 1986 NBA Finals.

mediocrity. Bird was limited by ankle and back injuries. And K. C. Jones, who had taken over as coach beginning with the 1983–84 season, retired after the 1987–88 season. The team remained strong but could not return to the Finals. Soon Bird, McHale, and Dennis Johnson retired.

In 1994, the Celtics missed the playoffs and finished with a losing record for the first time in 15 years. During the 1996–97 season, they compiled the worst record in franchise history at 15–67. From there, they suffered through eight straight losing seasons. But at the turn of the new century, the team had new players and new hope.

CHAPTER 5

THE BIG FOUR

T wo great players and an average defense is no formula for earning NBA titles. But four great players and a stifling defense is the recipe for winning championships.

The Celtics brought those facts into focus during the first decade of the 21st century. They spent nearly all six seasons from 1998–99 through 2004–05 hoping that the talented combination of guard Paul Pierce and forward Antoine Walker could lead the team to another title. The duo did guide the Celtics into the playoffs in 2002, 2003, and 2005. They even led a charge into the 2002 Eastern Conference finals. There Boston lost in six games to the New Jersey Nets.

Pierce and Walker simply did not have enough help. In fact, the pair combined for nearly half the team's points

Paul Pierce drives to the basket during a November 2001 game against the Washington Wizards.

THE FAMED FLOOR

While many other NBA teams were moving into new arenas in the 1970s and beyond, the Celtics had tradition on their side. They stayed in a home that was built in 1928.

The Boston Garden housed both the Celtics and the Boston Bruins of the National Hockey League. It was famous not only for the legendary sporting events that were played there, but also for its unique court. The Celtics played on a parquet floor, which looked like puzzle pieces cut into equal-size squares. The Garden floor was unlike any other in the NBA.

The Celtics moved into the Fleet Center—now known as TD Banknorth Garden—in 1995. To maintain tradition, that arena also features a multi-squared parquet floor. The Boston Garden was demolished in 1997.

from 2000 to 2003. Soon Walker was gone, and the Celtics had slipped toward the bottom of the NBA standings. Under second-year coach Doc Rivers, they fell to 33–49 in 2005–06 and a miserable 24–58 the next season.

General manager Danny Ainge yearned to return the team to its glory days. So after the 2006–07 season, he stunned the basketball world. He traded three players to the Seattle SuperSonics for All-Star guard Ray Allen. And he traded five players and two draft choices to the Minnesota Timberwolves for superstar forward Kevin Garnett.

The moves seemed risky. Both players were more than 30 years old. But Allen and Garnett had shown no signs of slowing down. Allen was still among the finest shooters in the league. And Garnett was a

Kevin Garnett, *center*, and Ray Allen, *right*, combined with Paul Pierce, *left*, to make Boston a championship contender again.

brilliant all-around player who could score, pass, defend, and rebound.

Going into the 2007–08 season, many basketball followers were predicting that the Celtics would win the title. But Rivers knew that championships are not won with talk. They are won by stopping opponents. So he summoned Garnett, Allen, and Pierce into his office before the season and made a speech.

"This is not going to work if you don't commit to playing defense, because we can't just be a good defensive team," he told them. "We have to be a great defensive team."

Rivers was right. And the Celtics indeed played amazing defense. The previous season, they had given up 99.2 points per game to rank 18th in the NBA. After trading for Garnett and Allen, they surrendered just 90.3 points per contest to rank second. Boston also compiled a league-best 66–16 regular-season record.

The Celtics were tested in the 2008 playoffs. They nearly lost to the Atlanta Hawks and the Cleveland Cavaliers in the first two rounds. The Celtics then ousted the Detroit Pistons in six games to advance to the NBA Finals. They were up against Kobe Bryant and the Los Angeles Lakers.

The Celtics won all three games in Boston, including a 131–92 success in Game 6, to claim their first championship in 22 years. Bill Russell and John Havlicek watched proudly from the sideline. When it was over, Garnett dropped to his knees and kissed the image of the Celtics' leprechaun mascot at center court. He had never before won an NBA championship.

"I got my own. I got my own," Garnett said to Russell. "I hope we made you proud."

"You sure did," Russell answered.

In the process, "the Big Three" had become "the Big Four." Boston point guard Rajon Rondo, just 22 years old, recorded 21 points, seven

Glen Davis, *right*, joined the Celtics as part of the trade to bring Ray Allen over from the Seattle SuperSonics.

rebounds, eight assists, and six steals in the Game 6 defeat of Los Angeles.

Those who believed the Boston team would soon be too old to contend for another championship were mistaken. With the same four players leading the way, the Celtics reached the NBA Finals again in 2010. They pushed the Lakers to the limit but lost 83–79 in Los Angeles in Game 7.

With the same core team, Boston bounced back for the 2010–11 season. They finished first in the Atlantic Division and third overall in the Eastern Conference.

After sweeping the New York Knicks in the first round of the playoffs, the Celtics

faced the Miami Heat. The Heat had made some big moves before the 2010–11 season. They signed LeBron James from Cleveland and forward Chris Bosh from the Toronto Raptors. Those two combined with Heat superstar Dwyane Wade to form Miami's own version of the Big Three.

Miami won the first two games of the series at home. The Celtics were able to win Game 3 in Boston to cut Miami's lead to two games to one. But the victory came with a heavy price. Rondo got tangled up with Wade and dislocated his elbow in the third quarter of the game. He played through the pain, but was not as effective. That injury, combined with the speed and athleticism of the Heat and

the age of the Celtics, helped Miami win the series four games to one.

Even though they did not make another trip to the Finals, Boston still had a strong team. With a combination of veteran leadership and young playmakers, the Celtics will still be a tough matchup for any team in the league.

Kevin Garnett celebrates winning his first NBA championship after Boston's 131–92 victory over the Lakers in Game 6 of the 2008 Finals.

TIMELINE

1946	The Celtics are founded on June 6 as part of the BAA under owner Walter Brown.
1949	Boston joins the NBA, the league created as a result of a merger between the BAA and the NBL.
1950	Arnold "Red" Auerbach is hired as the Celtics' coach and becomes one of the the most prominent non-players in NBA history. Boston signs point guard Bob Cousy, who helps transform the sport with his dazzling dribbling and passing.
1957	On April 13, the Celtics clinch their first league title with a 125–123 double-overtime victory over visiting St. Louis in Game 7 of the NBA Finals.
1962	On April 18, Boston wins 110–107 in overtime over the visiting Los Angeles Lakers in Game 7 of the Finals for the team's fourth consecutive title.
1965	On April 15, John Havlicek deflects a pass to clinch the Celtics' 110–109 victory over the visiting Philadelphia 76ers in Game 7 of the Eastern Conference finals. Radio announcer Johnny Most makes his famous "Havlicek stole the ball" call.
1966	On April 28, the Auerbach era ends in style as the Celtics win their eighth straight NBA championship with a 95–93 victory over the visiting Lakers in Game 7 of the Finals.
1976	The Celtics win Game 5 of the NBA Finals in triple-overtime over the Phoenix Suns before clinching the title in Game 6. The Celtics capture their second title in three years.

1979	After drafting him the previous year, Boston signs rookie forward Larry Bird to a five-year contract on June 8.
1986	The Celtics finish the season with a league-best 67–15 record before clinching the title. First-round pick Len Bias dies of a drug overdose on June 19, just two days after Boston drafted him.
1993	Boston star guard Reggie Lewis dies on July 27 after collapsing during an off-season workout. It is determined that Lewis had a heart defect that led to his death.
1995	The Celtics move from the famed Boston Garden to the brand-new Fleet Center, which is later renamed TD Banknorth Garden.
1997	On April 20, the Celtics hit rock bottom by completing a franchise-worst 15–67 season.
2004	On April 29, the Celtics name former standout NBA point guard Glenn "Doc" Rivers their new coach.
2008	The Celtics finish the regular season with an NBA-best 66–16 record and then defeat the Lakers in the Finals for their first title in 22 years.
2010	Led by "the Big Four" of Ray Allen, Kevin Garnett, Paul Pierce, and Rajon Rondo, the Celtics advance to their 21st NBA Finals appearance in team history. Los Angeles defeats visiting Boston 83–79 in Game 7.

FRANCHISE HISTORY

Boston Celtics (1946–)

NBA FINALS
(1950– ; wins in bold)

1957, 1958, **1959**, **1960**, **1961**, **1962**, **1963**, **1964**, **1965**, **1966**, **1968**, **1969**, **1974**, **1976**, **1981**, **1984**, 1985, **1986**, 1987, **2008**, 2010

CONFERENCE FINALS
(1971–)

1972, 1973, 1974, 1975, 1976, 1980, 1981, 1982, 1984, 1985, 1986, 1987, 1988, 2002, 2008, 2010

KEY PLAYERS
(position[s]; years with team)

Larry Bird (F; 1979–92)
Bob Cousy (G; 1950–63)
Dave Cowens (C/F; 1970–80)
Kevin Garnett (F; 2007–)
John Havlicek (F/G; 1962–78)
Tom Heinsohn (F/C; 1956–65)
Dennis Johnson (G; 1983–90)
Sam Jones (G/F; 1957–69)
Ed Macauley (C/F; 1950–56)
Kevin McHale (F/C; 1980–93)
Robert Parish (C; 1980–94)
Paul Pierce (F; 1999–)
Bill Russell (C; 1956–69)
Bill Sharman (G; 1951–61)
Jo Jo White (G; 1969–79)

KEY COACHES

Red Auerbach (1950–66):
    795–397; 91–60 (postseason)
Tom Heinsohn (1969–78):
    427–263; 47–33 (postseason)
K. C. Jones (1983–88):
    308–102; 65–37 (postseason)

HOME ARENAS

Boston Garden (1946–95)
TD Banknorth Garden (1995–)
    —Known as Fleet Center
    (1995–2005)

*All statistics through 2010–11 season

QUOTES AND ANECDOTES

"We knew we were going to win. It was just a question of how we were going to embarrass the other team." —Guard Rick Carlisle, on the 1986 NBA champion Celtics

The 1970s and 1980s Celtics had some colorful nicknames. Dave Cowens was known as "Big Red" because of his height and red hair. Fellow Hall of Fame center Robert Parish was called "The Chief" because he resembled a character of that name from the famous 1975 movie, *One Flew over the Cuckoo's Nest.* But forward Cedric "Cornbread" Maxwell owned perhaps the strangest nickname of all. He received it from college teammate Melvin Watkins after the two saw a movie titled, *Cornbread, Earl and Me.*

Players and fans did not really need the final seconds to tick off the game clock to know the Celtics had clinched another victory. They could just look over at Red Auerbach. As both coach and general manager, Auerbach lit a fat cigar when he believed the game was won.

"Red Auerbach is the best coach in the history of professional sports, period." —Former star center Bill Russell, on the legendary Celtics coach

In 1989, Celtics president Red Auerbach received a letter from a fourth-grade teacher in Louisiana. She wrote that her students had been learning the capital cities of states in the Northeast. She asked one student if he knew the capital of Massachusetts. The boy thought about it for a while, and then blurted out, "Celtics!"

GLOSSARY

assist
A pass that leads directly to a made basket.

contract
A binding agreement about, for example, years of commitment by a basketball player in exchange for a given salary.

draft
A system used by professional sports leagues to select new players in order to spread incoming talent among all teams. The NBA Draft is held each June.

dynasty
A team that dominates a particular league or sport for a period of time.

fast break
A style of basketball in which a team runs down the court and tries to score before the opponent defense is set.

franchise
An entire sports organization, including the players, coaches, and staff.

free agent
A player whose contract has expired and who is able to sign with a team of his choice.

general manager
The executive who is in charge of the team's overall operation. He or she hires and fires managers and coaches, drafts players, and signs free agents.

playoffs
A series of games in which the winners advance in a quest to win a championship.

rebound
To secure the basketball after a missed shot.

rival
An opponent that brings out great emotion in a team, its fans, and its players.

trade
A move in which a player or players are sent from one team to another.

FOR MORE INFORMATION

Further Reading

Hubbard, Donald, with Jo Jo White. *100 Things Celtics Fans Should Know & Do Before They Die*. Chicago: Triumph Books, 2010.

Reynolds, Bill. *Rise of a Dynasty: The '57 Celtics, The First Banner, and the Dawning of a New America*. New York: NAL Hardcover, 2010.

Simmons, Bill. *The Book of Basketball: The NBA According to the Sports Guy*. New York: Random House, 2009.

Web Links

To learn more about the Boston Celtics, visit ABDO Publishing Company online at **www.abdopublishing.com**. Web sites about the Celtics are featured on our Book Links page. These links are routinely monitored and updated to provide the most current information available.

Places to Visit

Naismith Memorial Basketball Hall of Fame
1000 West Columbus Avenue
Springfield, MA 01105
413-781-6500
www.hoophall.com
This hall of fame and museum highlights the greatest players and moments in the history of basketball. Larry Bird and John Havlicek are among the many former Celtics who have been inducted.

TD Banknorth Garden
100 Legends Way
Boston, MA 02114
617-624-1050
www.tdbanknorthgarden.com
This has been the Celtics' home arena since 1995, when it was known as the Fleet Center. The team plays 41 regular-season games here each year.

The Sports Museum
100 Legends Way
Boston, MA 02114
617-624-1234
www.tdbanknorthgarden.com/sportsmuseum
Located inside TD Banknorth Garden, the Celtics' home arena, this museum highlights the rich history of sports in Boston, including the achievements of the Celtics.

INDEX

About the Author

Marty Gitlin is a freelance writer based in Cleveland, Ohio. He has written more than 35 educational books. Gitlin has won more than 45 awards during his 25 years as a writer, including first place for general excellence from the *Associated Press*. He lives with his wife and three children.